# Emmanuel CHABRIER

## ESPAÑA
*Rapsodie pour orchestre*
(1883)

Edited by
Clinton F. Nieweg
Nancy M. Bradburd

**Study Score**
Partitur

SERENISSIMA MUSIC, INC.

# Chabrier

## España
Rapsodie pour Orchestre

Published Sources:

Score: Enoch Frères et Costallat éditeurs, Paris, Version originale par Grand orchestre,
    plate E.F. & C. 891, n.d. [1884], 61 p. [Also published in study score size, plate 891].
Parts: Enoch Frères et Costallat éditeurs, Paris, plate E.F. & C. 892, n.d. [1884].
Parts: Edward B. Marks Music Corp., NY, Hampton Orchestra Library, Hol-20.
    Reprint of the Enoch parts with handwritten changes.
Score: Edwin F. Kalmus, NY, 1933, Boca Raton, FL, 1989, 61 p.
    Reprint of the above score and parts. Published in Full and Study size.
Study score: Ernst Eulenburg Ltd., London, plate E.E. 6018, 1953, No. 893, 72 p.
    Foreword by Maurice Cauchie.
Reduced orchestra: Enoch & Cie., Paris, plate E. & C. 3426, n.d.[1897], 78 p.
    réduction pour orchestra ordinaire par Gabriel-Marie, score
2 Piano score: Enoch Frères & Costallat éditeurs, Paris, plate E.F & C. 893, n.d. [1884], 32 p.
    Transcription pour 2 pianos par l'auteur. Reprint : E.F. Kalmus, NY n.d. (later Belwin)
Piano solo: Enoch & Cie., Paris, plate E.F. & C. 896, n.d. [1884].
    Transcription de Concert pour piano seul par C. Chevillard, score, 17 p.
Piano 4 hand score: Enoch Freres & Costallat, Paris: plate E.F. & C. 894, n.d. [1884], 25p. also Enoch & Sons, London, [1925]. Réduction pour piano à 4 mains par A. Messager.
Chabrier: livre bilingue, francais/anglais / [édité] par Roger Delage [Genève]: Minkoff & Lattes, ©1982,
    211 p. chiefly ill. (some colored).

*España, Rhapsody pour orchestre* was completed in 1883, the World Première was on (4?) or 6 November of that year at the "Societé des nouveaux concerts", conducted by Charles Lamoreux. The Societé was founded in 1881 and is a long-established and beloved presence in French music. Led since 1993 by the Japanese-born phenomenon Yutaka Sado, the Orchestre Lamoureux is closely identified with many important French orchestral works, including Ravel's Valses *Nobles et Sentimentales* and Chabrier's *España*, both of which were premiered by the orchestra. Ravel himself led the orchestra in the first recording of his *Bolero* in 1932. The American première of *España* was given by the Philharmonic Society of Boston at the Boston Music Hall on January 14, 1884, Bernard Listemann, conducting.

Emmanuel Chabrier's family intended him to become a lawyer, and as such, he worked in the Ministry of the Interior for eighteen years. But his passion was always music, and he began composing on the side, publishing many minor works and two operettas before finally abandoning his ministry post in 1880 to devote his time to composition.

It was *España* that established Chabrier as a composer of serious works. In 1882, he visited Spain with his wife and family and was enchanted by the energy of Iberian music. Returning to Paris, he promised the conductor Charles Lamoureux he would write a Spanish-themed piece that would cause audience members to leap up and embrace each other. Though the first performance in 1883 may not have ended in a group hug, the piece did catch fire with the public and its themes were so memorable that the main melody was a hit again 73 years later in a 1956 ditty called *Hot Diggity* by Hoffman and Manning.

Though he first wrote *España* for piano, Chabrier quickly realized it needed the thrust and brilliance that orchestration could give it. Written in the traditional sonata form, the two main themes contrast the tempestuous Spanish jota with the slower, lyrical malagueña. In the development, Chabrier hints at the "endless variety of rhythms" that he heard superimposed on the basic 3/4 pattern of the dance. A new theme is introduced by the trombones, punctuated by references to the opening theme. The conventional recapitulation is followed by a coda bringing back the trombone theme for a brilliant conclusion.

# Comments Regarding Disparities between Original Enoch Score and Parts

**Composer:** Chabrier, Emmanuel  **Title:** España Rapsodie pour Orchestre

Original Publisher: Enoch  Publisher: Edwin F. Kalmus, LC., © 2008

The printed Enoch score does not match the engraving of the original Enoch parts in the notation of the articulations, dynamics and some notes in this work. Many of these have been added to this corrected edition as they appear in the original parts. The Enoch parts had some handwritten changes made in the reprint by Hampton Music Library which then appeared in the 1933 Kalmus reprint.

Due to the instrumental forces required in the Bassoon, Trumpet and Harp sections, cues for important lines for Bassoons 3 and 4, Cornet 2 and Harp 2 have been placed into the parts of like instruments. In this way, the piece can be performed with two bassoons, three trumpets and one harp.

| Status Code | Instrument | Enoch Rehearsal System | Measure Number | Beat | Comment |
|---|---|---|---|---|---|
| | | | | | Score = The original Enoch score; Parts = the original Enoch parts. |
| | Trombone 1, 2 | Entire part | | | Score: Tenor clef. The original part has the pitches correctly in tenor clef but the margin of each line was engraved with an alto clef! |
| | Cello | Measures 13 to 16 | 13 to 16 | | Score: Note C on beats 1&3; 2; 1&3; 2. Part: Note C on beats 2; 1&3; 2; 1. This edition uses the score notation matching the Viola rhythm. |
| | Cornet 2 | 17 | 17 | | Throughout this edition the Cornet 2 is cued into the Trumpet 1 or 2 or Cornet 1 or Trombone 1 parts when possible. |
| | Bassoon 3, 4 | A; −4 | 25, 26 | 2, 3 | Throughout this edition the Bassoon 3 and/or 4 are cued into the Bassoon 1, 2 (or Trombone 3 or Tuba) parts when possible. |
| | Woodwinds | A; 34 | 61 | 2 | Score *fff*. Parts *ff*. |
| | Clarinets | B; −1 | 77 | | Score: *tr~~* on each measure. Part: continues *tr~~~~* from measure 77 to measure 93. |
| | Oboes | B; −1 and +2 to 14 | 79 to 91 | 2 | Score: has accents. Parts: have *sf*. |
| | Timpani | B; 19 etc. | 96 etc. | 2 | Score and Parts: Rolls were notated with the older method using 4 beams. In this edition the modern notation of 3 beams has been used for all Timpani and Percussion rolls. |
| | Harp 2 | B; 19 etc. | 96 etc. | 3 | Harp 2 passages have been cued into Harp 1 whenever playable. Some Harp 2 passages must be omitted if only one harp is available. |
| | Harp 1, 2 | B; 19, 20 etc. | 96, 97 etc. | | Score and parts have a *crescendo* sign. Measures 104, 105; 316, 317; 324, 325 are marked to be simile using the crescendo. |
| ? | Tambourine | B; 21, 29 | 98, 106 | 1 | 16th note added in this edition as in Enoch score measure 318 (5 measures after I) and measure 326 (13 measures after I). |
| | Harp 1 | B; 31 | 108 | 1 | Score and Part: *f*. The similar measure 328 has mf (I; measure 15) in |

| Status Code | Instrument | Enoch Rehearsal System | Measure Number | Beat | Comment |
|---|---|---|---|---|---|
| | | | | | Score = The original Enoch score; Parts = the original Enoch parts. |
| | | | | | the Score and Part. The mf reading is used in this edition. |
| | Clarinets, Bassoons | C; 31 | 144 | | Score: beats 1 and 2 are slurred. Clarinet parts: beats 2 and 3 are slurred. Bassoon parts: no slur printed. This edition matches the Clarinet parts and measure 160 (2 measures before D). |
| | Trumpets | E; 3, 4 and 7, 8 | 194, 195 and 198, 199 | | Score: no articulation in measures 194 to 195. Slur in measures 198 to 199. Parts: staccato on C, slur D to C, staccato on G for both phrases. This edition uses the contrast of accented Cornets, then slurred Trumpets from 192 to 199 (E; 1 to 8). |
| | Oboe 1 | D; 6, 7 | 167, 168 | | Score: rests. Part: dotted eighth note A to eighth note B. Not added to this edition. |
| | Strings | D to E and K, etc. | 162 to 191 and 366 to 393 | | This edition shows both the Enoch phrasing as corrected and practical bowings. The Enoch Score and Parts contain numerous differences in the printed phrasing. |
| | Trombone 1, 2, 3 | E; 10 | 201 | 3 | Score: whole measure rest. Original part: eighth note F/Ab/Db chord notated. Hampton edition part: whole measure rest. |
| | Timpani | E; 10, 12 | 201, 203 | 3 | Score: whole measure rest. Part: eighth note F on beat 3. |
| | Violin 2 | F; 38, 40, 42, 44 | 245, 247, 249, 251 | 1 | Score: an F eighth note is printed on every beat 1. Part: every 2 measures an eighth rest is printed on beat 1. |
| | Basses | F; 39 to 43 | 246 to 250 | | Score: Arco. Part: Pizz. Arco used for this *ff* passage. |
| | Clarinets | F; 48 to 51 | 255 to 258 | | Score: dotted eighth notes printed. Part: has rests. |
| | Flutes, Clarinets | H; 1 to 9 | 281 to 289 | | The phrasing in this edition matches the Enoch Clarinet parts and the piano edition. |
| | Piccolo | I; 5 to 8<br>I; 13 to 15 | 318 to 316<br>326 to 328 | | The pitches in the original score are notated like Flute 2 (sounding $8^{va}$). The pitches in the original part are notated like Flute 1 (sounding $8^{va}$). This edition uses the notation found in Flute 1 sounding $8^{va}$. See also measures 98 to 101 (B; 21 to 24) and 106 to 108 (B; 29 to 31). |
| | Tambourine | I; 5, 13 | 318, 321 | 1 | Score: $16^{th}$ note. Part: rests. Editorial $16^{th}$ note added to measures 98 & 106 (B; 21 & 29) for the same musical pattern. |
| | Harp 1 | J; 14 | 347 | 1 | Score: Right hand chord C,G,Bb,C. Part has C,E,Bb,C. |
| | Oboe 1 | J; 15 | 348 | 1 | Score has B. Part has A. Solo piano edition has A. This edition uses the reading of the note A from the part, as it fits the chord in the piano edition. |
| | Timpani | K; 4, 12 | 369, 377 | | This edition adds the final C of the phrase. See measure 165 (D; 4) and measure 173 (D; 12). |
| | Cello | K; 7, 8 | 372, 373 | | Upper line: Tie added to a middle C as in measures 168, 169 (D; 7 & 8). |
| ? | Timpani | K; 19, 21 | 384, 386 | | Score and Part: The written note is F. If a third drum is used a G can be played when it fits the bass line harmony. |
| | Oboe 1, 2 | K; 20 | 385 | 3 | Score has C. Part has D. Piano edition has C. |
| ? | Violin 1, Clarinet 1 | K; 40 | 405 | 3 | Enoch score has Concert G in clarinet 1 and a note that could be read G or A in the Violin 1. Enoch Violin 1 part has A; Clarinet 1 part has Concert A. This edition uses the Concert G to create the G7 |

| Status Code | Instrument | Enoch Rehearsal System | Measure Number | Beat | Comment |
|---|---|---|---|---|---|
| | | | | | Score = The original Enoch score; Parts = the original Enoch parts. |
| | | | | | chord as in the composer's arrangement for 2 pianos, 4 hands. |
| | Tempo | L; 1 | 408 | | Score: *Serrez peu à peu le mouv*. Parts: *Poco più mosso*. |
| | Horn 3, 4 | L; 1 etc. | 408 etc. | | For the notation of the concert C in Bass clef the score used "old notation". This edition uses the modern notation. |
| | Bassoon 2 | L; 11 | 418 | 2, 3 | Score and Part have the note F. Solo Piano edition has E. |
| ? | Brass | M; – 4 to M | 435 to 438 | | Score: measures 435 to 438 (4 before M to M) have no articulation, except for one accent on Trombone 1 (measure 437 beat 1). Parts: A mixture of accents, staccati, forzando signs are found. Piano edition has forzando signs (^). |
| | Clarinets | M; 13 to 16 | 451 to 454 | | Score: notated as in this edition. Parts: Clarinet 1 unison with Oboe 2. Clarinet 2 melody now printed in Clarinet 1. |
| | Flute 2, Piccolo | M; 17 to 20 | 455 to 458 | | Score: *tr~~* on each measure with ties. Part: continues *tr~~~~* from measure 455 to measure 458. Same for Flute 1 measure 459 to 462 (M; 21 to 24) |
| | Horn 1 | N; 11 to 13 | 481 to 483 | | Score and Part: Written G (Concert C). Piano edition has Concert F a 5th lower. Chabrier may have re-voiced this chord when preparing the orchestration. |
| | Viola | O; 1, 2 | 491, 492 | | Score: F and Bb double stop. Part: F and D. See measures 495, 496 (O; 5, 6). This edition uses the F and D double stop as in the original part. |
| | Violin 2 | O; 7 | 497 | 1, 2 | Score: double stops A,C; A,F; A,F; A,G. Part: notes A,C,F,G. |
| | Harp 2 | O; 7 | 497 | 3 | Score: The lowest note of the chord is A. Part: The lowest note is F which fits the bass line in that octave. |
| | Harps 1, 2 | O; 9 to 12 | 499 to 502 | | Score: Four note Chord on beat 1 and then notes on beat 2, 3. Parts: The parts have a triad spread out over the 3 beats of the measure. This edition uses the reading in the original parts. |

Compiled by Clinton F. Nieweg and Nancy M. Bradburd, 2008

**Status codes:** ? – editorial correction; conductor's decision

*We are indebted to Peter Conover, Principal Librarian, Chicago Symphony and Quelani Penland, Orchestra Librarian, UC Berkeley for allowing the study of original Enoch material.*

*The editors wish to acknowledge David J. Miller for his exceptional engraving work in creating this corrected edition.*

*The editors welcome any additions, corrections, or comments to this edition. Contact: proofferr@yahoo.com*

# ORCHESTRA

Piccolo

2 Flutes

2 Oboes

2 Clarinets (B-flat)

4 Bassoons

4 Horns (F)

2 Trumpets (F)

2 Cornets (B-flat)

3 Trombones

Tuba

Timpani

Percussion

(Bass Drum, Cymbals, Triangle, Tambourine)

2 Harps

Violin I

Violin II

Viola

Violoncello

Double Bass

Duration: ca. 7 minutes

Premiere: November 4, 1883
Paris, Théâtre du Château d'Eau
Societé des nouveaux concerts
Orchestra, Charles Lamoreux (conductor)

ISMN: 979-0-80000-151-2
ISBN: 978-1-932419-956-6

© Copyright 2008 Clinton F., Nieweg, Nancy M. Bradburd.
Previously issued by E.F. Kalmus as A1368.

# España
## Rhapsody for Orchestra

EMMANUEL CHABRIER
Edited by Clinton F. Nieweg
and Nancy M. Bradburd

SERENISSIMA MUSIC, INC.

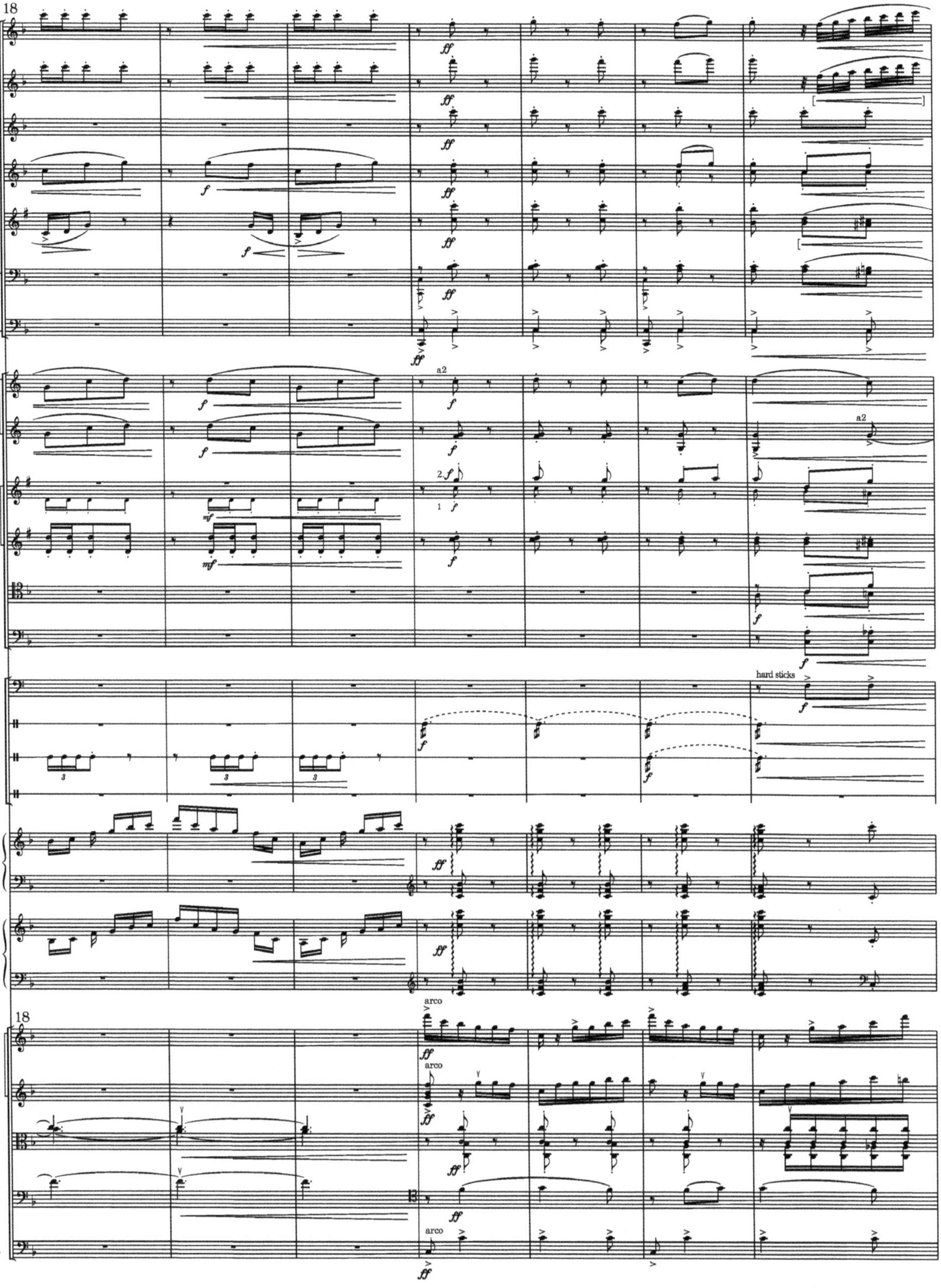
18
Picc.
Fl. 1 2
Ob. 1 2
Cl. 1 2
Bn. 1 2 3 4
Hn. 1 2 3 4
a2
Tpt. 1 2
Cnt. 1 2
Tbn. 1 2
Tbn. 3 Tuba
Timp.
hard sticks
Tgl.
Tamb.
Cymb. B. D.
Hp. 1
Hp. 2
18
Vn. I II
arco
Va.
Vc.
Cb.

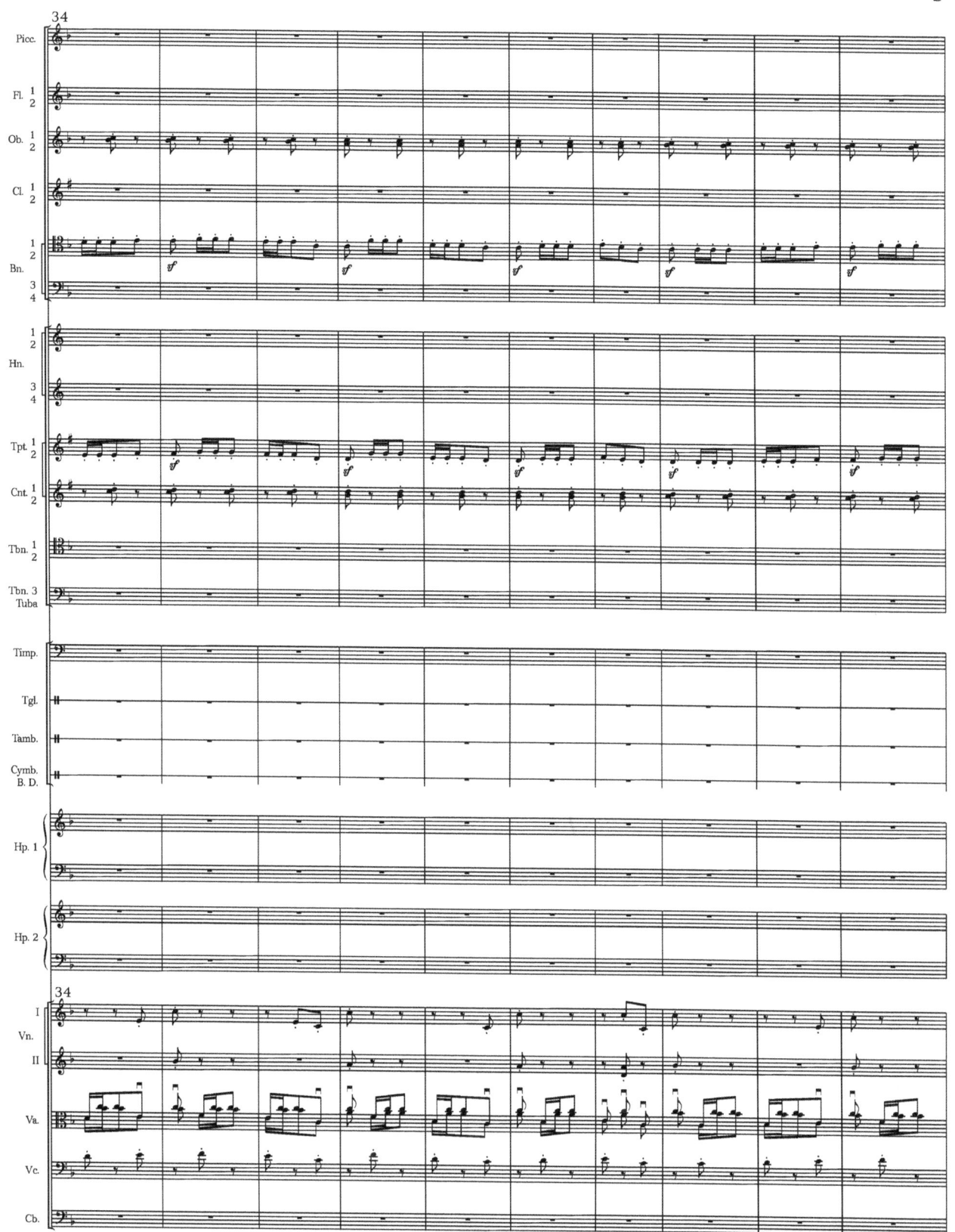

8

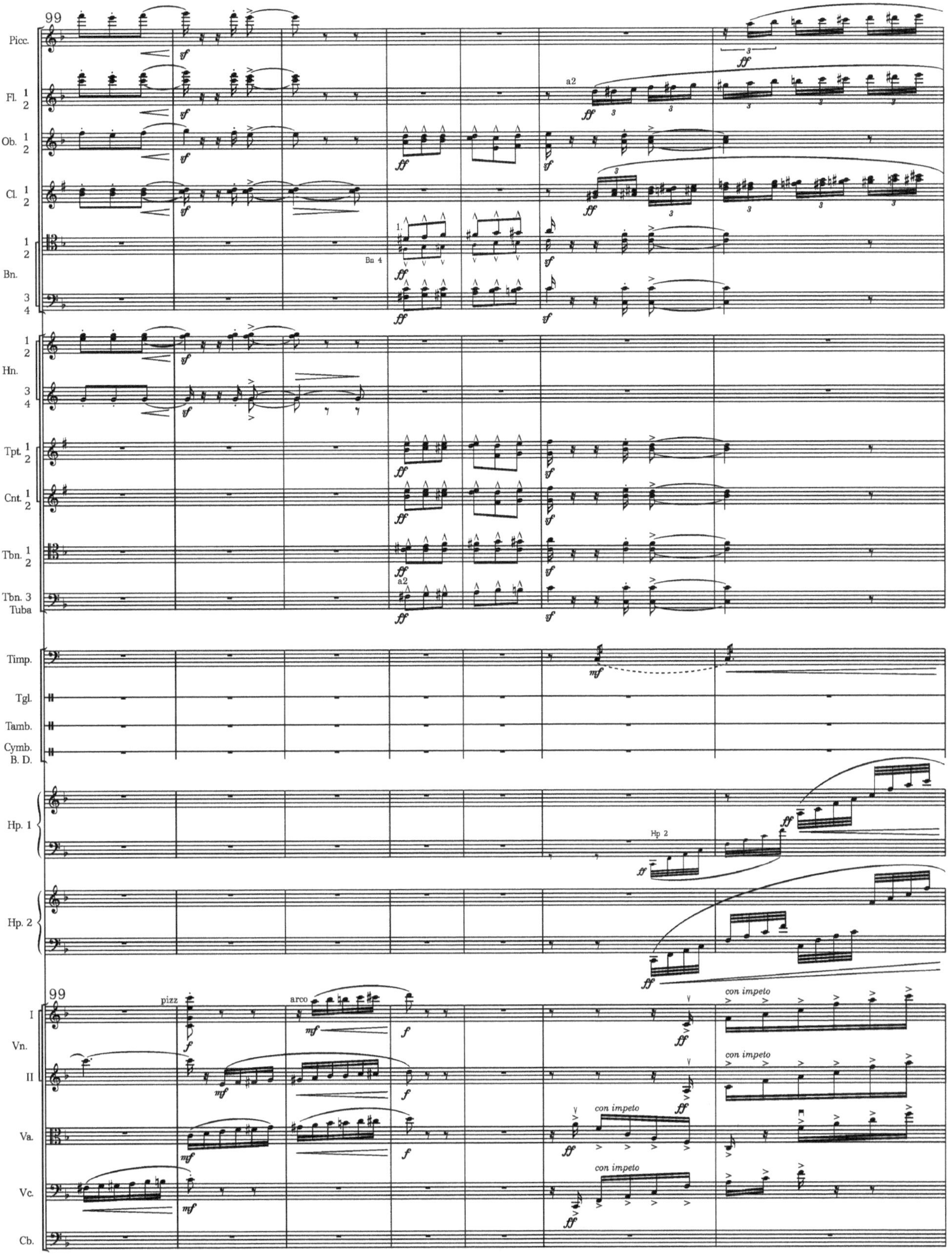
99
Picc.
Fl. 1 2
a2
Ob. 1 2
Cl. 1 2
Bn. 1 2 3 4
Bn 4
Hn. 1 2 3 4
Tpt. 1 2
Cnt. 1 2
Tbn. 1 2
Tbn. 3 Tuba
a2
Timp.
Tgl.
Tamb.
Cymb. B. D.
Hp. 1
Hp 2
Hp. 2
99
Vn. I II
pizz
arco
con impeto
Va.
Vc.
Cb.

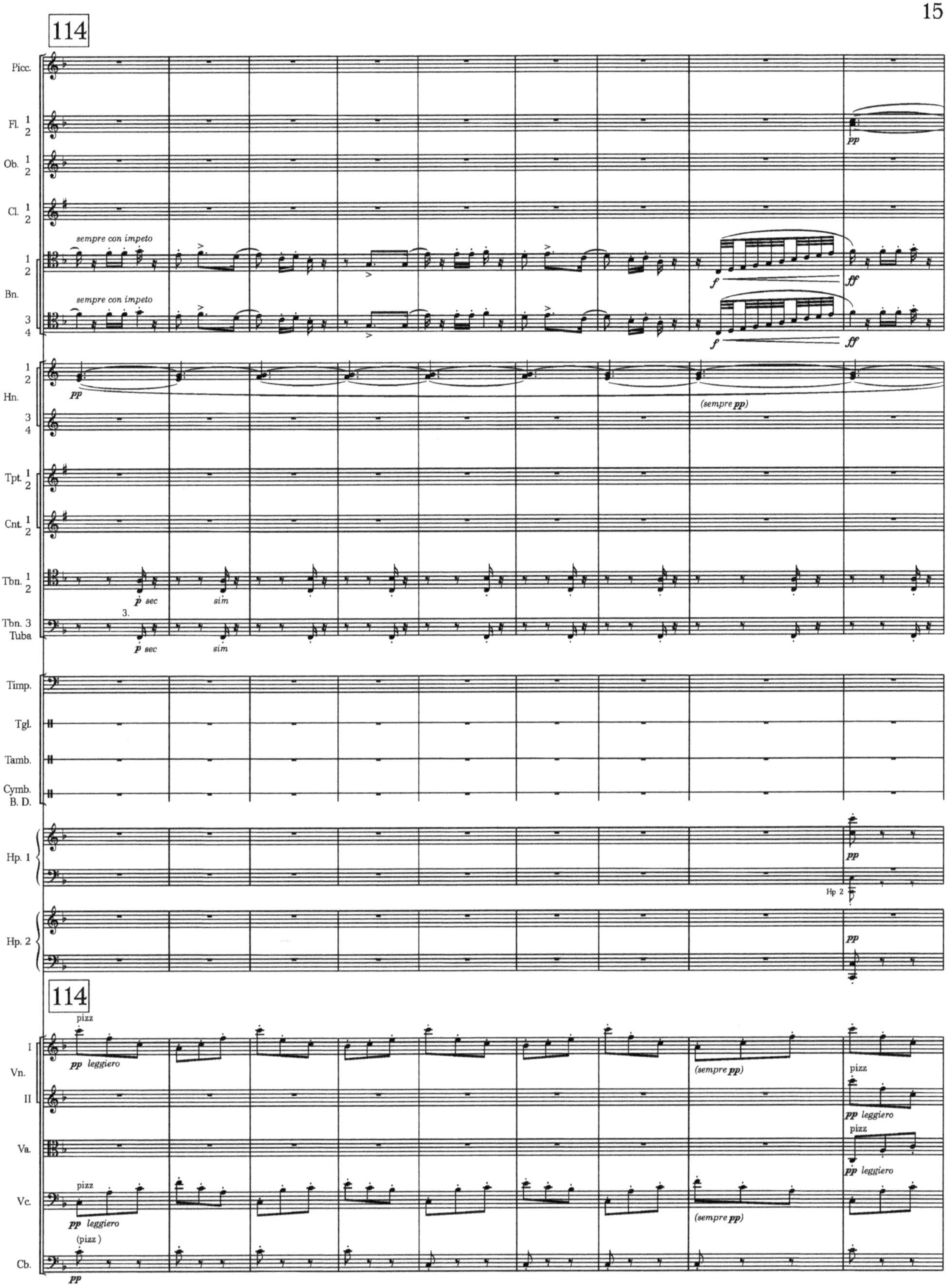
114
Picc.
Fl. 1 2
Ob. 1 2
Cl. 1 2
Bn. 1 2 3 4
sempre con impeto
pp
ff
Hn. 1 2 3 4
(sempre pp)
Tpt. 1 2
Cnt. 1 2
Tbn. 1 2
Tbn. 3 Tuba
p sec
sim
Timp.
Tgl.
Tamb.
Cymb. B. D.
Hp. 1
Hp. 2
Hp 2
114
Vn. I II
Va.
Vc.
Cb.
pizz
(pizz )
pp leggiero
(sempre pp)

16

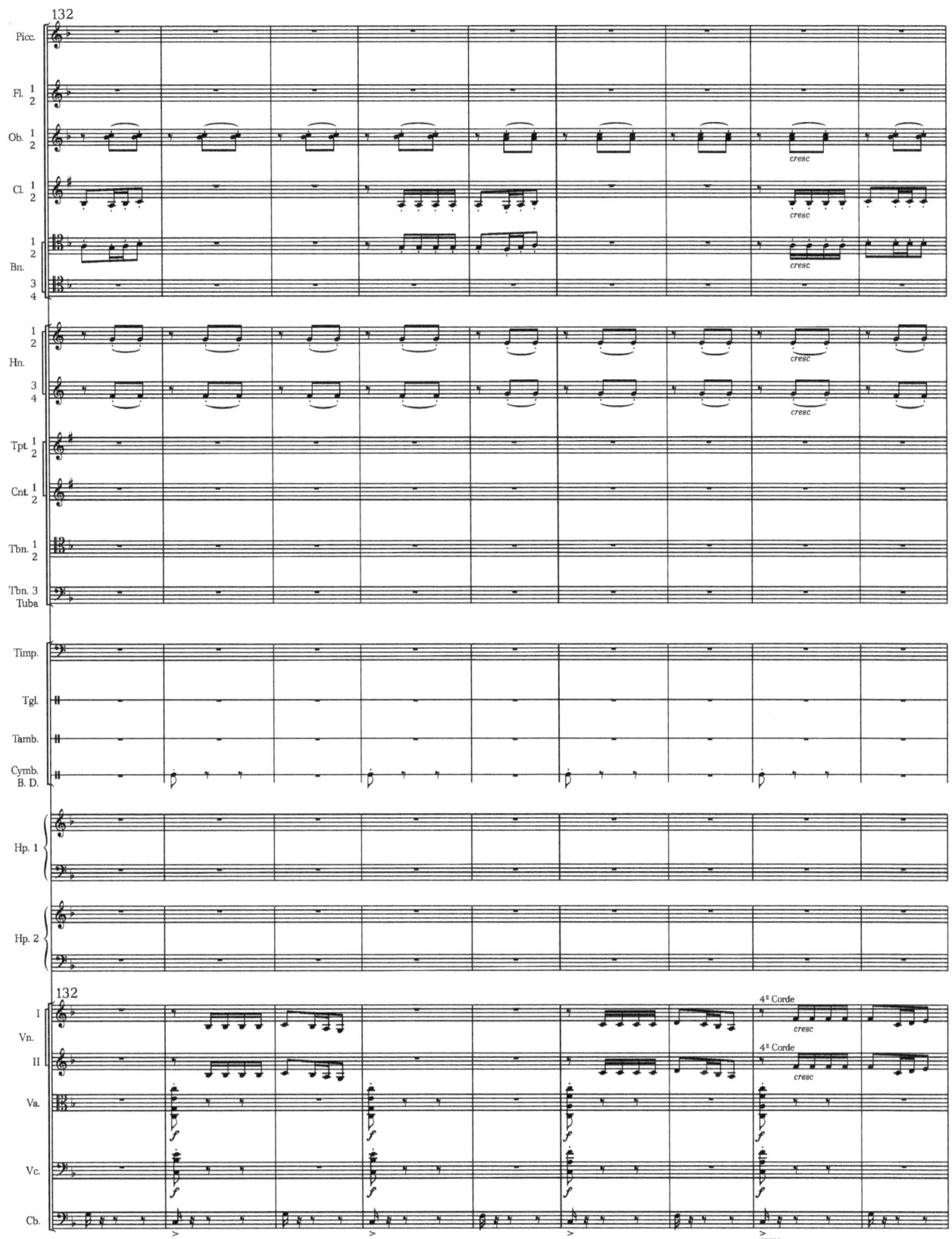

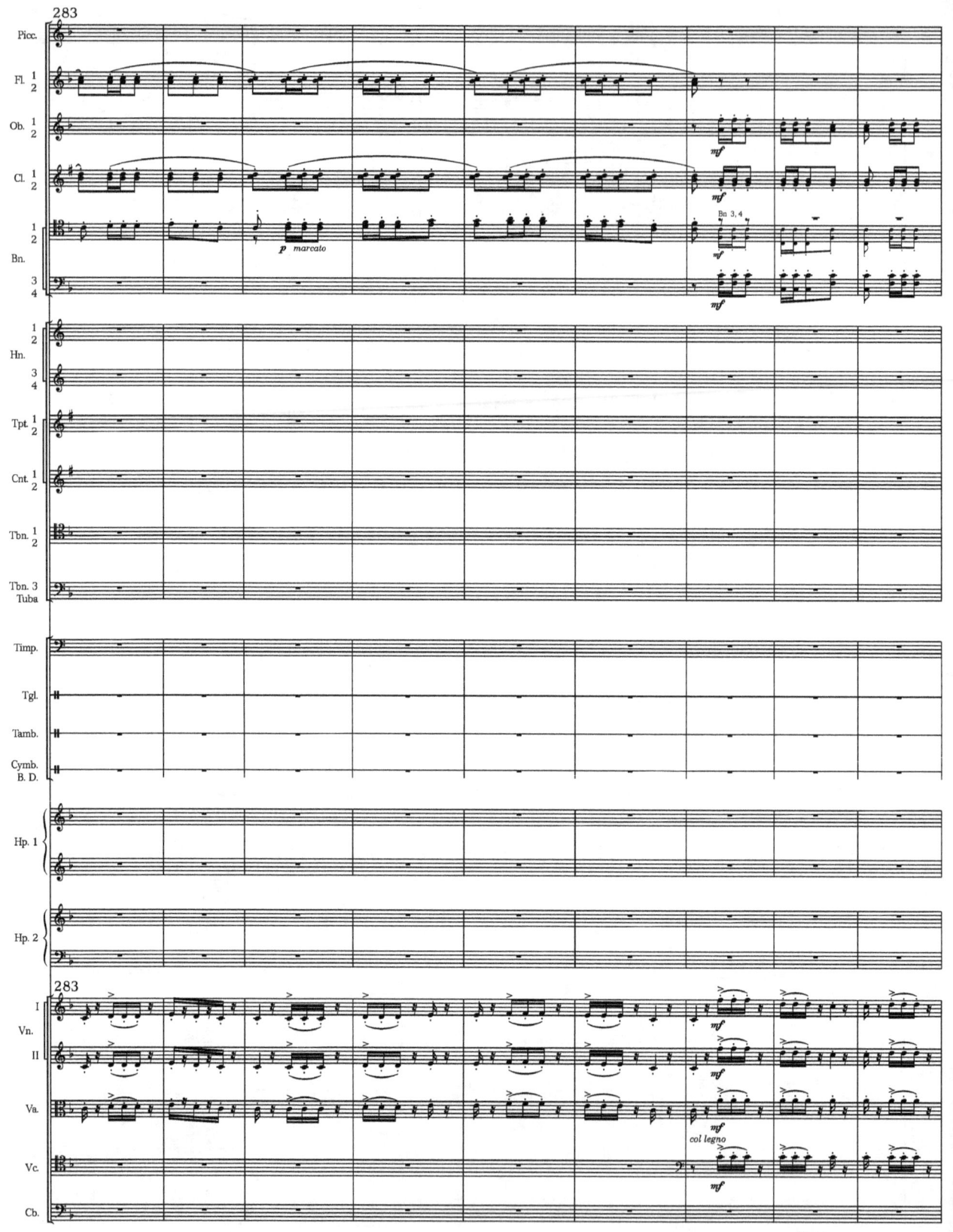

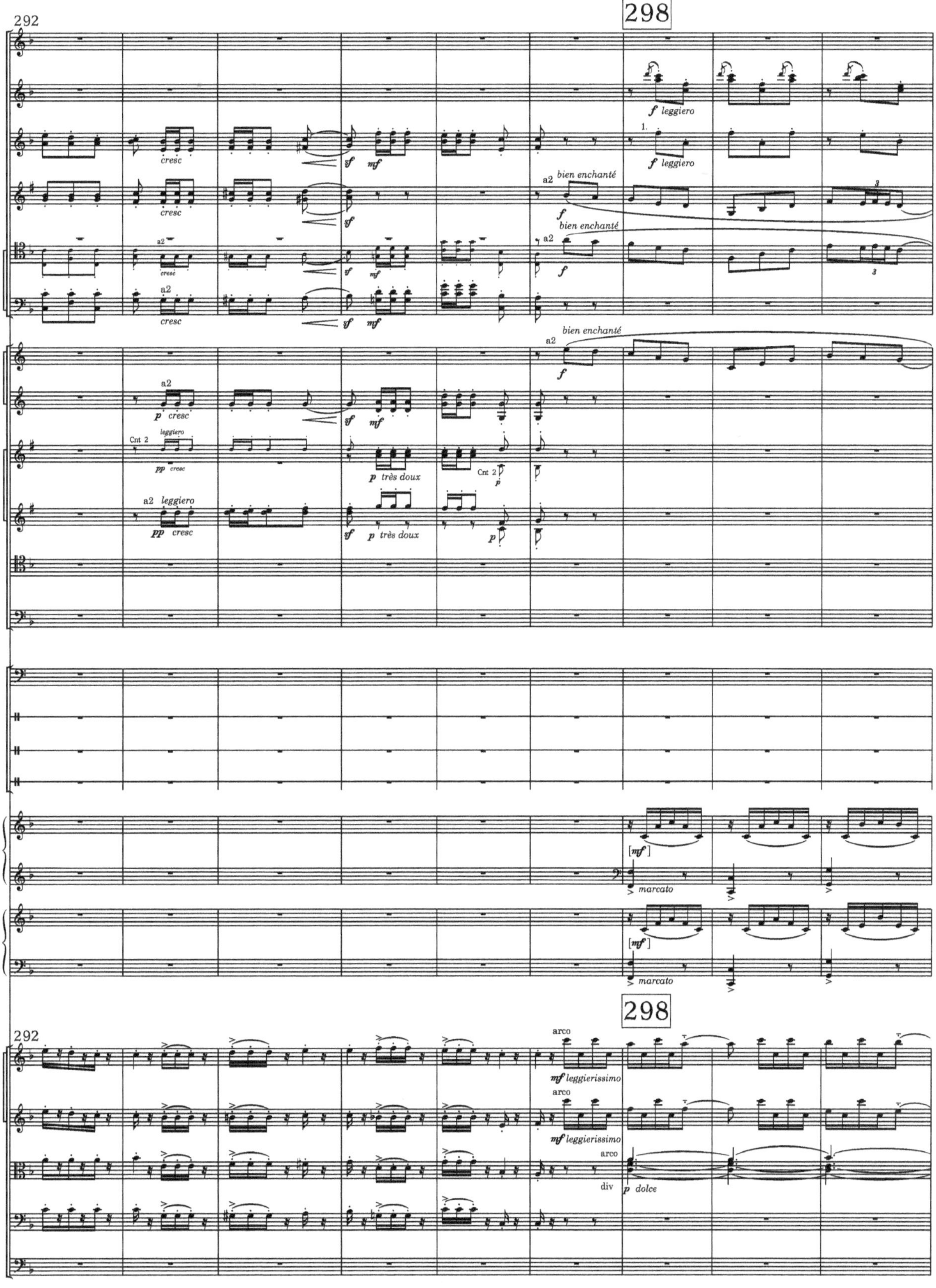

292
298
Picc.
Fl. 1 2
Ob. 1 2
Cl. 1 2
Bn. 1 2 3 4
Hn. 1 2 3 4
Tpt. 1 2
Cnt. 1 2
Tbn. 1 2
Tbn. 3 Tuba
Timp.
Tgl.
Tamb.
Cymb. B. D.
Hp. 1
Hp. 2
Vn. I II
Va.
Vc.
Cb.
cresc
a2
bien enchanté
f leggiero
1.
p cresc
Cnt 2
leggiero
pp cresc
p très doux
a2 leggiero
[mf]
marcato
arco
mf leggierissimo
div
p dolce

38

40

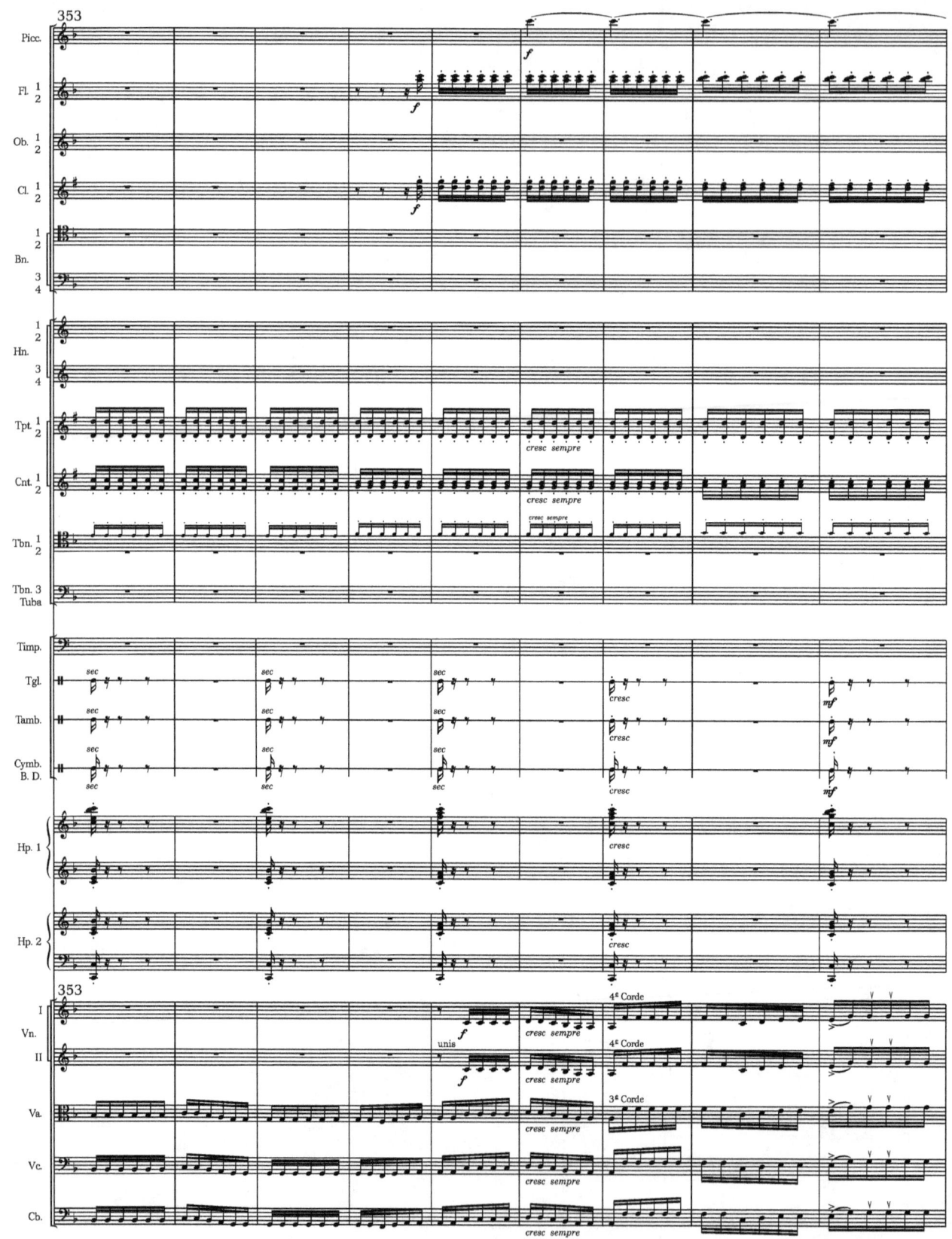

46

48

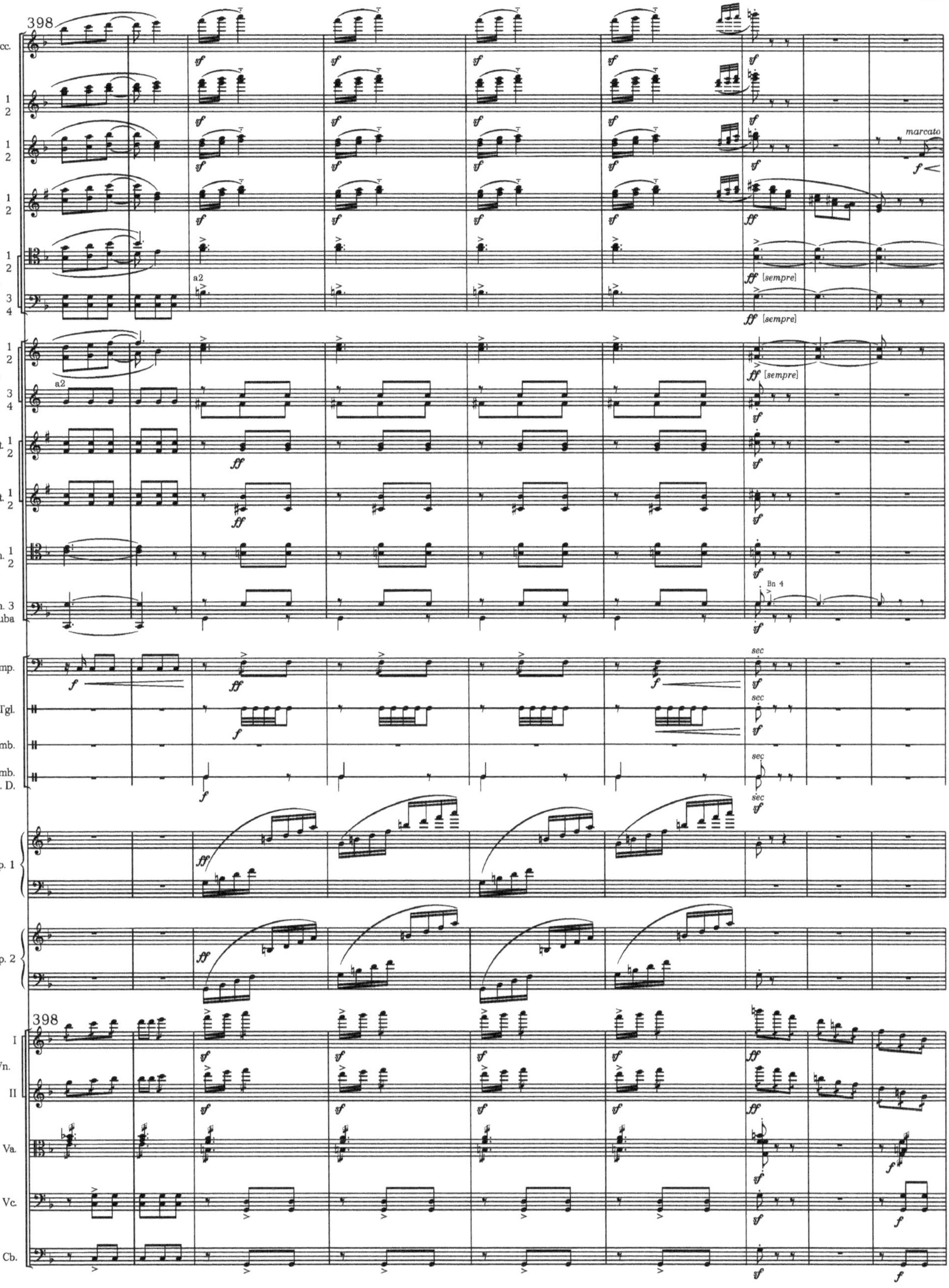
398
Picc.
Fl. 1 2
Ob. 1 2
marcato
Cl. 1 2
Bn. 1 2 3 4
a2
ff [sempre]
Hn. 1 2 3 4
Tpt. 1 2
Cnt. 1 2
Tbn. 1 2
Tbn. 3 Tuba
Bn 4
Timp.
sec
Tgl.
Tamb.
Cymb. B. D.
Hp. 1
Hp. 2
398
Vn. I II
Va.
Vc.
Cb.

53

www.ingramcontent.com/pod-product-compliance
Lightning Source LLC
Chambersburg PA
CBHW081356040426
42451CB00017B/3467